Animal Camouflage in the Ocean

Hidden in Nature

by Martha E. H. Rustad

Consulting Editor: Gail Saunders-Smith, PhD
Consultant: Tanya Dewey, PhD
University of Michigan Museum of Zoology

Capstone press

Mankato, Minnesota

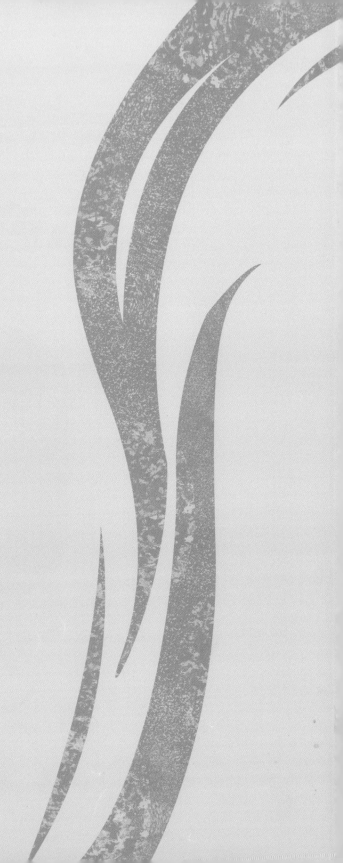

Pebble Plus is published by Capstone Press,
151 Good Counsel Drive, P.O. Box 669, Mankato, Minnesota 56002.
www.capstonepress.com

Books published by Capstone Press are manufactured with paper
containing at least 10 percent post-consumer waste.

Library of Congress Cataloging-in-Publication Data
Rustad, Martha E. H. (Martha Elizabeth Hillman), 1975–
    Animal camouflage in the ocean / Martha E.H. Rustad.
    p. cm. —— (Pebble Plus. Hidden in nature)
    Includes bibliographical references and index.
    Summary: "Simple text and photographs present animals that are camouflaged in the ocean" — Provided
by publisher.
    ISBN 978-1-4296-3325-3 (library binding)
    1. Marine animals — Juvenile literature. 2. Camouflage (Biology) — Juvenile literature. I. Title. II. Series.
QL122.2.R87 2010
591.47'2 — dc22   2009007305

Editorial Credits
Erika L. Shores, editor; Abbey Fitzgerald, designer; Svetlana Zhurkin, media researcher

Photo Credits
Alamy/WaterFrame, 17
Getty Images/Science Faction/Michele Westmorland, 13
iStockphoto/Dan Schmitt, 1; Tommy Schultz, 5
NOAA/Dr. Dwayne Meadows, NOAA/NMFS/OPR, 21
Peter Arnold/Tim Rock, 11; Wolfgang Poelzer, 9
Seapics/Shedd Aquar/Edward G. Lines Jr., 15
Shutterstock/David E. Heath, 7; Filip Fuxa, cover; John A. Anderson, 19

Note to Parents and Teachers

The Hidden in Nature set supports national science standards related to life science. This book
describes and illustrates animal camouflage in the ocean. The images support early readers
in understanding the text. The repetition of words and phrases helps early readers learn new
words. This book also introduces early readers to subject-specific vocabulary words, which are
defined in the Glossary section. Early readers may need assistance to read some words and to
use the Table of Contents, Glossary, Read More, Internet Sites, and Index sections of the book.

Table of Contents

In the Ocean 4

Hiding in Ocean Reefs 8

Hiding on the Ocean Floor . . . 14

Glossary 22

Read More 23

Internet Sites 23

Index 24

In the Ocean

In *the* a wet world,

animals need to blend in.

Camouflage helps

ocean animals hunt

or stay safe.

Jellyfish have clear bodies.

They blend in everywhere.

Jellyfish can sneak up
on prey and sting them.

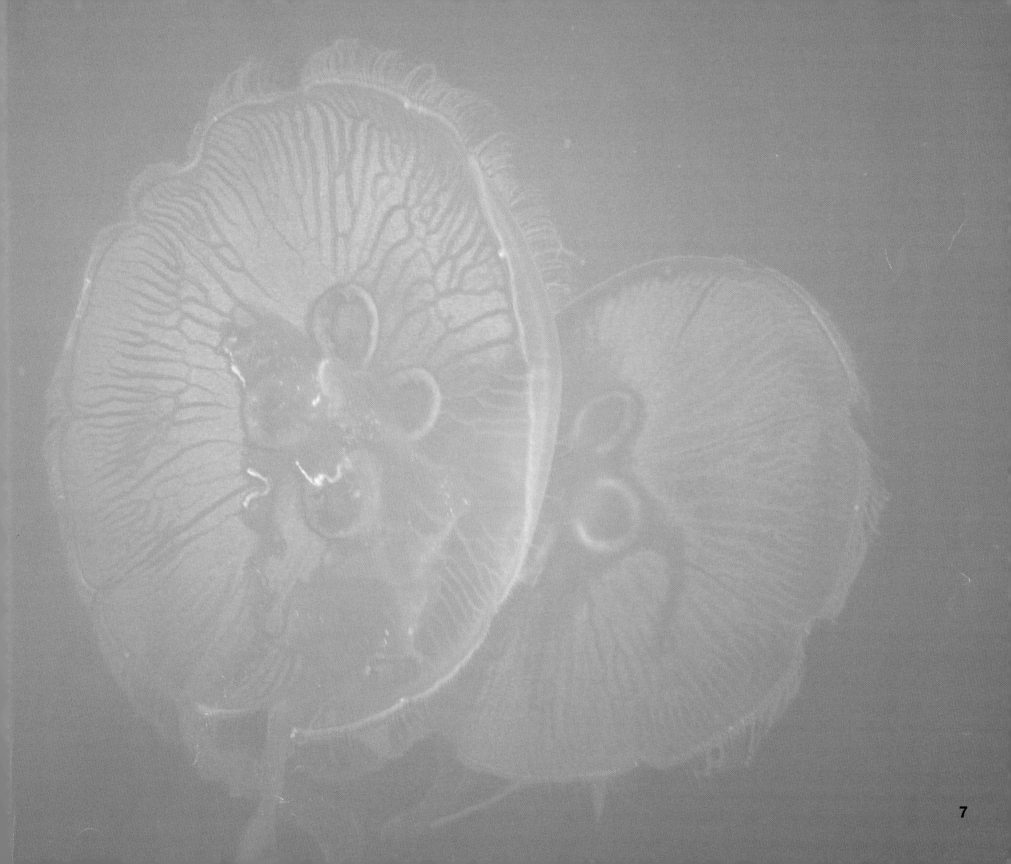

Hiding in Ocean Reefs

Sea horses hide from predators.

This sea horse has bumpy,

pink and white skin.

It looks like coral.

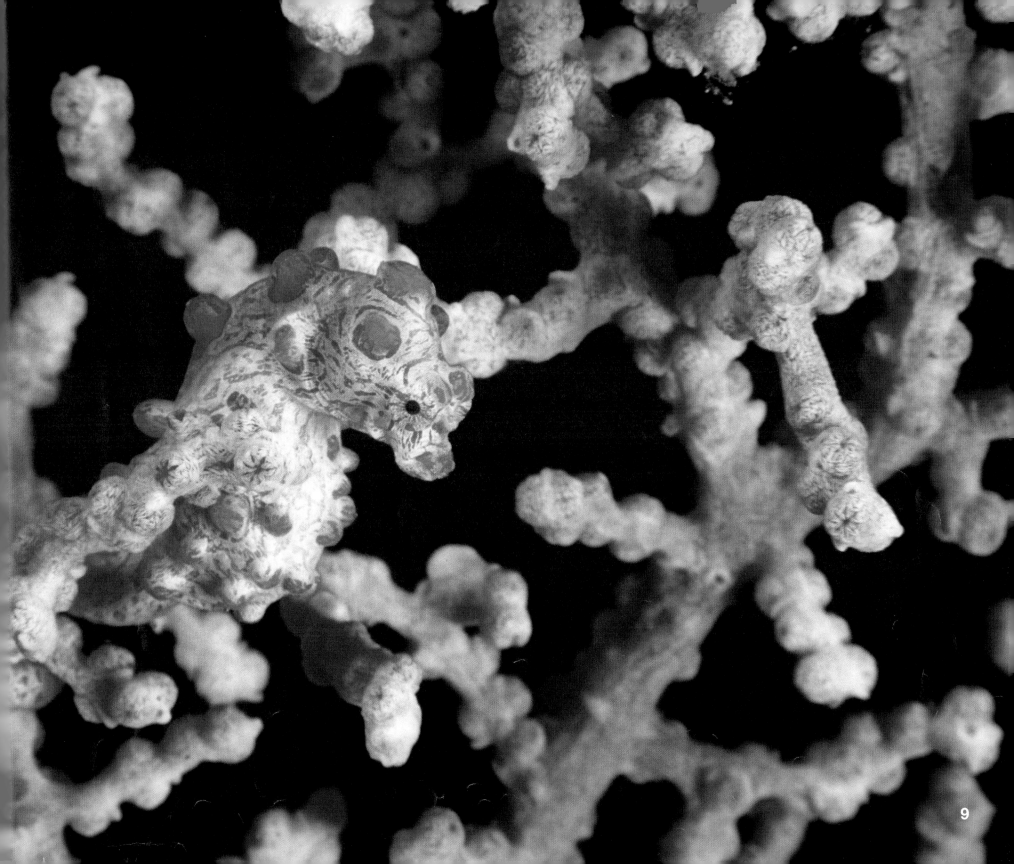

Skin that changes color

hides octopuses on coral.

Sharks can't spot them.

Some shrimp have red
and white bodies.
They match the coral
where they live.

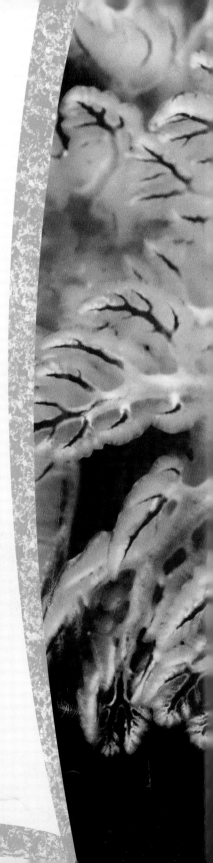

Hiding on the Ocean Floor

Rays swim along the ocean floor.

Brown and yellow spots hide

this ray from predators.

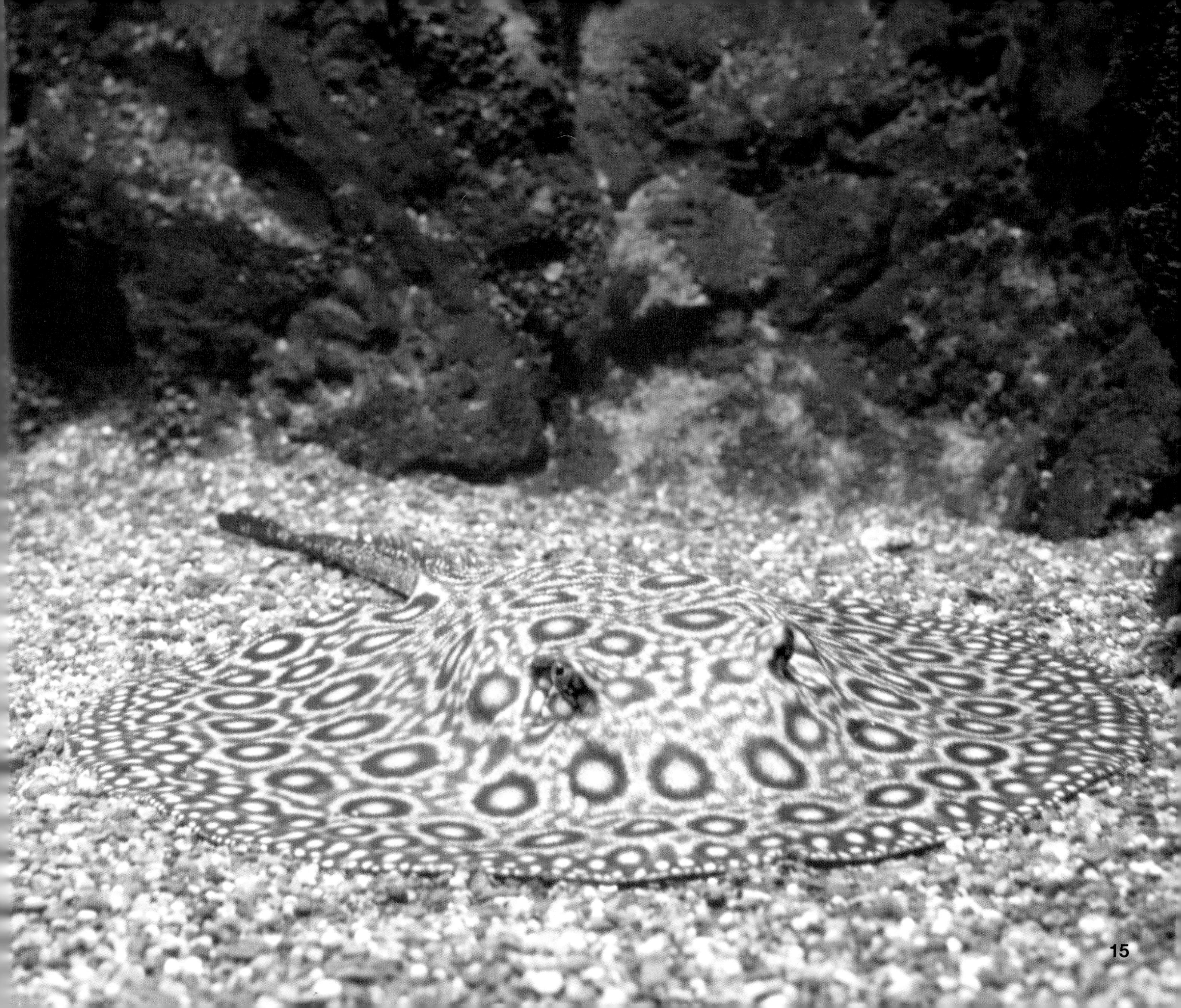

Sea stars have bumpy skin
that matches their surroundings.
Sea stars stay safe in the sand.

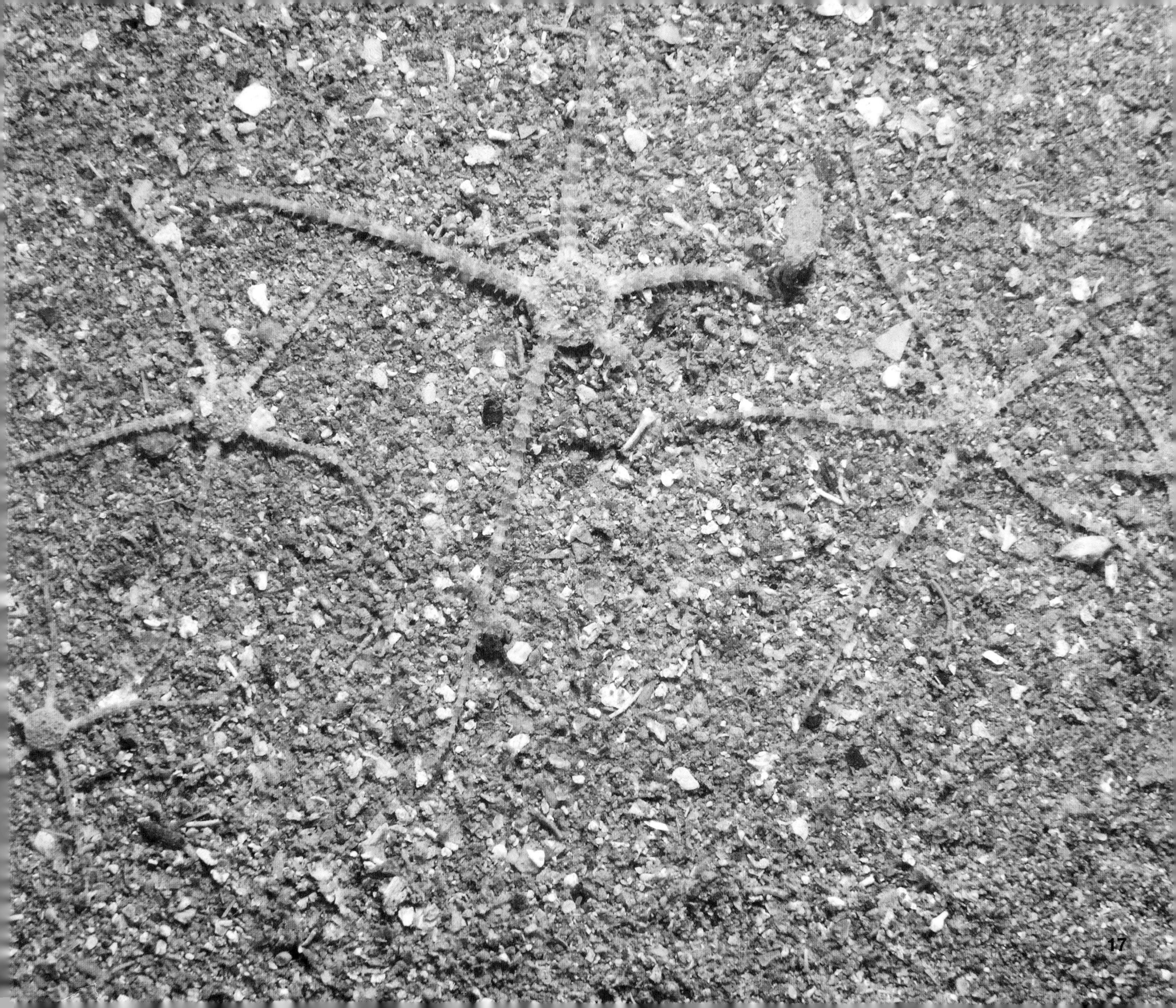

17

Pipefish have striped skin
and long bodies.

They hide on the ocean floor.

Predators can't spot flounders.
Bumpy, brown skin hides
these fish in ocean sand.

21

Glossary

camouflage — coloring or covering that makes animals look like their surroundings

coral — tiny ocean animals that live together in huge groups called colonies; corals join their bodies together and attach to coral reefs.

predator — an animal that hunts other animals for food

prey — an animal hunted by another animal for food

Read More

Armentrout, David, and Patricia Armentrout. *Crafty Critters.* Weird and Wonderful Animals. Vero Beach, Fla.: Rourke, 2009.

Salzmann, Mary Elizabeth. *What Has Spots?* Creature Features. Edina, Minn.: Abdo, 2008.

Internet Sites

FactHound offers a safe, fun way to find Internet sites related to this book. All of the sites on Facthound have been researched by our staff.

Here's all you do:

Visit *www.facthound.com*

FactHound will fetch the best sites for you!

Index

coral, 8, 10, 12
flounders, 20
hunting, 4
jellyfish, 6
ocean floor, 14, 18
octopuses, 10
pipefish, 18
predators, 8, 14, 20
prey, 6
rays, 14

safety, 4, 16
sand, 16, 20
sea horses, 8
sea stars, 16
sharks, 10
shrimp, 12
skin, 8, 10, 16, 18, 20
spots, 14
stinging, 6

Word Count: 135
Grade: 1
Early-Intervention Level: 18